About the Author

I completed an MA in Creative Writing at the University of Portsmouth in 2019. I live in Hampshire opposite the sea with my teenage daughter, Anisa and our Westie, Millie.

Melanie Hope, MA, MSc

Hotchpotch

Melanie Hope

Hotchpotch

Olympia Publishers
London

www.olympiapublishers.com
OLYMPIA PAPERBACK EDITION

A CIP catalogue record for this title is
available from the British Library.

ISBN: 978-1-78830-808-3

First Published in 2021

Olympia Publishers
Tallis House
2 Tallis Street
London
EC4Y 0AB

Printed in Great Britain

Dedication

For all the people I love and for all the people who love me.
You know who you are.

Acknowledgements

With thanks to the Creative Writing MA team at the University of Portsmouth – all staff and students.

Many thanks to my friend, Lucinda Bothwell, for her brilliant front cover design.

Youth of Today

With your memes and your flix
And your peng, best selfie pics.
And your branded clothes – blazon advert,
Bright, ripped, slogan T-shirt.

No paper, no pens,
Definitely no book ends.
Wi-fi, and laptops,
Glad-eye for crop-tops.

Energy drinks, pint sinks,
Happy slaps, back-to-front baseball caps.
Large portion of chips,
Eying up any pouty lips.

Sees a gig, or two or twenty,
Has Instagram followers; more than plenty.
Ear or fingers stuck to the phone
Hears the latest score on the way home.

What a generation, how insane,
Living lives in the super highway lane.
Social media, podcasts, software creations,
Replacing books and face-to-face conversations.

Bric-a-Brac Attack

Ladder climb with slipper soft steps,
Expanse of attic heaps aplenty – linger of dusty fust.
Everything here including a kitchen sink –
Algae green around the plug hole.
A one-stringed guitar with a pile of sheet music.
A spindle-legged spider sits on a treble clef.

A scramble over the bric, a clamber over the brac.
Pile of newspapers – the colour of used coffee filter paper.
A doll – fright of hair – sits by her disjointed arm.
Teddy with a Cheshire smile; dapper in a tartan waistcoat –
Upright and waiting for adoption.

Stained duvet; history of tumbles, fumbles
And feverish mumbles.
Flexless kettle; plug torn – wisp fray of wires.
Wedding dress – a touch of the Havershams.

A rusty sandwich maker, draped with a skipping rope;
Piles of football programs – from United's glory days.
Binbags of old clothes – a shudder of eighties shoulder pads,
And day-glo nineties.

A chunky hunk of junk ready for the bin bags;
Stacks of memories destined for a car boot.

Cape Town 1951

Hetty unlocked the cabinet.
The porcelain doll with expression vague, blue eyes glazed;
Titchy hands holding layers of tuile and lace.
Hetty traces dolly's taut lips with her black finger.

Dolly's hair wasn't crinkled, her skin wasn't tar.
If she was like dolly, her hair brush would slide,
And the white boys wouldn't gangle monkey chants
From that upstairs window.

A sudden rush of Sister Mary-Rose.
Grabs the doll, snatches the key, and secures her back in the glass case.
No words, no explanation.
Hetty's world slides into further disappointment.

Valentine

Giggles behind hands, girls in short-skirted uniforms, ties absurd in size,
Flick through cards: oblongs, squares, padded
And a few the size of tabloids.
Get that one; get that one, or that. Get all three.

A suit reaches for a card for Marion,
Who has a black cat.
Card has a small black puss picture. Suits the suit.
Turns it over to check the price.

Track-suits gather for a garrulous decision.
Shoulder-jump, posture point at a saucy card for Jasmine.
Snigger and back-slap;
Try to outdo each-other's volume.

Counter lady watches over the top of her specs.
She's never had a valentine's card.
Lives with her cat Evelyn.
Has a ready meal for tea.

Mad for Dogs

Small ones, shy ones,
Hot under the collar ones.
Feisty and fly ones.
Tongue-lolloping drool ones.
Pointy pointers and whippety whippets.
Cocker poos and pretty doggy mixtures.
Hairy ones, and slidey-glidey ones.
Ginormous shaggy dog ones.
You are the best. With your slobber and
Boisterous ardour; your sniffles,
Snuffles and paw-muffles,
Your energetic loyal lovingness.

You smell of you, of home, and love.
I adore you all.

Woman's Best Friend

When daddy died, you knew.
You tilted your fluff-head to one side,
And threw a wet-eyed stare
And you held it there for some time.

Slowly, you walked towards me
Head hung low with respect,
And lay the side of your face on my knee
And you held it there for some time.

A tear crawled and landed on my lap
And I reached into the cardboard box for a tissue.
And you knew little dog.
How did you know?

The PM and The President (Thank you to Edward Lear for The Owl and the Pussycat)

The PM and the President were all at sea
With news that is hard to quote.
They took your money, yes all your money.
Wrapped up in bought for vote
The Pres looked up to the stars afar
And sang to a small guitar,
'Oh lovely PM, oh PM, my dear,
What a super PM, you are,
You are,
You are!
What a super PM you are!'

PM said to the Pres, 'You elegant trowel,'
How alarmingly sly is this thing!
We work well, like we're married; too long we have tarried:
Call me – yes give me a ring?'
They plugged away, for a year and a day,
To the place where the money tree grows.
And there as they would, a large banker stood
With a wad to end all their woes,
Their woes,
Their woes,
With a wad to end all their woes.

'Dear Sir, are you willing to sell for small billing
More shares?' said the banker, 'I will.'
So they took papers away, and were minted next day,

By the wodge that their great laps did fill.
They dined ever since on slices of quince,
Which they ate with a big silver spoon;
And hand in hand, with the sound from a band,
They danced, not too soon,
Oh yes,
They danced, not too soon,
Not too soon.

Top Banana

So unappealing.
Smell like a bin, look like you're riddled with a malignant melanoma.
Peel your outer garment, shed tendrils of slime, and pull them away more
Appear.

So fru-fru with three squishes of squirty cream. There's no glory in you, or
Knickers or bocker. And that glacé cherry is a joke. It's the red nose on a
Yellow clown.

You always make your way onto slices of sarnie bread,
And I've seen Andy Murray noshing on you at Wimbledon.
I've seen you swim with custard. What's the point of that?
No one cares because you shed your skin on the floor and trip them up.
Bad banana.

You Fell off the Wall

Mrs Hawkin's garden smells of new cut grass.
Auntie splits daisy stalks with her thumb nail,
To make chains,
And you were sitting on the high, brick wall.

You sudden-screech; pull a stupid gurn of a face.
Lots of rush, and unfamiliar blood gush.
Nobody smiles, or notices me.
Went to play in the greenhouse.

Inside was a tiny ceramic house, grey and crumbly.
Wood lice lived there. They scuttle in
And scurry out like they had stuff to do.
So I put the roof back on to protect their privacy.

My brother was back with a Mr Bump plaster,
And a ninety-nine.
I will fall off the wall tomorrow,
So I can have the same.

If Poker Deals
(With thanks to Rudyard Kipling's If)

If only you can keep your cool when all about you
Are losing theirs and blaming it on you,
If you can trust your gut instinct when others are watching you,
But flip the next card for the next break through.
If you can wait and stay patient by waiting,
Or wait for David's fold and hear his sighs,
Or being baited, don't give way to baiting
And yet don't look too assured, just avert your eyes.

If you can dream-and not make dreams your master;
If you can think- and make a twist your aim;
If you can meet with triumph and not disaster
And treat these next two moves the highlight of your game;
If you can bear to see the risks you're taking
Twisting knaves to make a trap for fools,
And watch to see if they are faking,
And sweep and clean up with your top trump tools.

If you can make a pile of all your winnings
And risk all on one turn with a diamond toss,
And lose, and start again at your beginnings
And don't lose breath; don't care about the loss;
If you can force their hand with all the guts that's in you
To serve your turn when others are long gone,
And so hold on when you think you're through
Except your will, which says to you: 'go on!'

If you can play the crowds and keep your virtue,
Or work your kings - and use your slight, your touch,
If neither twist or sly unfurl can hurt you,
If all men can fold but you, it's all too much;
If you can fill that unbelievable last minute
With sixty seconds' worth of the glorious last run,
Yours is the world and everything that's in it,
And – what is more – you'll be the Man, my son!

Seaside Snapshot

The lick of waves advances, and retreats with suck-shingle and leaves a foamy flounce on the sea's indigo skirt. Gentle drags of salty glisten coats ribbons of seaweed slime.

In a sink of shingle underfoot, a little girl fills a plastic yellow sandcastle with a rattle-mix of stones, shells and grit. Her tongue, blue from a lolly-lick, covers her bottom lip with concentration.

Mother sits on a towel emblazoned with the Jamaican flag. She lays a striped cushion on Montego Bay. Remembers
the dental appointment is tomorrow. Shuffle-settles on her back.

Shimmer sea broken by an Alsatian pant; his vigorous sea-shake splashes the enormous beer-belly of a tentative swimmer as he tests the water with cream toes.

Sky stretch broken by occasional cloud billow, a squawk of seagulls swoop and screech. Eager to make their presence known. Eager to provide a soundtrack. Most definitely eager.

And the Winner is…

I will stand at the Oscar ceremony, coyly accept my first Oscar, first of many I hope. Laughter from the audience.

Shake my head, and blow.
Pause and shake my head again.

Didn't expect this, so haven't written anything. Glance at Oscar.
Kiss it, and then hold it aloft and lean into the podium. I thank the academy, the director Baz. See you for the sequel Baz. More laughter from the audience. My fellow actors, in particular, my co-star, Daniel, who was so generous. Love you Dan. My husband, who is the love of my life, and who, without whom, none of this is possible. My Mum and Dad who gave me the belief that anything is possible. My teacher, Brenda Hawkes, who told me to dream big and never give up. And finally, to my friend, Kate. I love you darling.

Whoops and cheers from the audience, as they stand and clap.

I lift my skirts and teeter off the stage.

Might happen.

Fly Away

Sits on a stout burst of a suitcase;
Struggle to strap; strains to shut.
Dad fancies a pint. Mum says it's 6.30 in the morning.
Daughter pouts selfies; son texts with both thumbs.

Flights delayed. All of them. All boarding gates empty.
All planes grounded. All miniature drinks firmly screwed.
People slumped on seats or asleep on the floor; backpacks for pillows
Children play chase between piles of baggage.

Mum visits duty free. Wheels through aisles.
A massive Toblerone rivalling the clink of trolley bottles.
Comes back reeking of perfume spritz,
Stripes of tester lipstick on her forearm.

Sudden panic to view an update.
Flight number 626 now boarding.
Rush to the departure lounge.
Drag of the cabin cases.

Fluster for the boarding passes.
Squeeze past the welcome of the cabin crew.
All set for sea, sunburn, heartburn, squabbles
Sangria and sickness. Happy holiday.

Sounds of Summon

The band.
Marching brass bands; visions of conflict and uniform.
Stir and drum up, trenches and gun whistle and mud-flick.
In the name of waving flag and country service. Turn right.
Attention, whack of rifle change; thump of glory drum.

The siren.
Sirens scream trauma and distress.
We are coming for you. Coming now.
We will throw up the ladder, throw out the stretcher, throw on the handcuffs
You will be safe, shielded, held.

The drill.
Fire drills camaraderie as we troop to the meeting point. leave
Bags, files or computer screens or shopping carriers. Don't know how long
We will be in the shiver or the rain. We quiver and squeeze arms, but laugh
And crack a joke. Or pat the arm of a late arrival.

Halloween

Ding dong

A shy witch – face green; lisps trick or treat.
As she scatters the sweety tin,
Smiling mother behind, reminds her to say thank you;
Mouths thanks as she guides her shoulders.

Ding dong

Boys bursting with energy, armed with eggs and flour.
Tricks they scream. Ready for the spite; eager for some damage.
One ten-year-old, hollow-eyed, and neck-bolted, splats an egg,
Slide of yellow yolk at the front bay.

Ding dong

Girls gothed with black lipstick, caked in fake.
Giggle through braces.
Skirts hitched, black lips.
Indifferent to the treats; eager for attention.

Halloween Ball

With a stiff gait and outstretched arms,
Franki ducks his huge, furrowed forehead.
Exposes his sleeves too short; his arms too stiff,
Joins the throng of ghouls and spectres on the dance floor.

A ghost and a spider jive; Spidey's legs flail and whack passers,
On their way to the caldron bubbling spread.
With a flaming finger buffet; drift of blood wine cocktails.
Watched over by a smiling gap-toothed pumpkin.

Dracula bows to a black-laced Morticia, and leads her to the dance floor.
Several black cats congregate around a devil; all of a simper.
And a wizard mans the decks; caresses the vinyl;
Creates a magic sound of throng song for the motley crew.

A werewolf and a mummy tango across the floor,
Narrowly missing the low-slung chandeliers festooned with cobwebs.
And as the clock strikes twelve and the dry ice rises
Skeletons syncopate with vampires in top hats with a timely Time Warp.

Love the Smell of You

Vanilla in a tiny bottle; the essence of you.
Just the chance to nose the delectable sweet-warmth:
It's cheesecake, or sticky French patisserie bake.

And yes. Fresh cut, fresh baked, crisp-crumbed bread.
So seductive, slaver of you;
Lashings of butter-ooze, and dollops of gooey-berry jam.

And you coffee, ay caramba, with your natty cups. Some wide and
Welcoming offer Cappuccino, others tight-lipped Espresso;
Aroma tantalises the air with the roast of you.

And rubber. The sniff of you. The snug-bug cosy of a hot-water bottle;
Memories of Santa, and brushed-cotton p-jays
And Dad's hair-smoothing lullabies.

Old churches with generations of soft candle-flicker, prayer-whisper.
Still, people-fill calm. The scent of human embrace
And life-affirming grace and hope of you.

Tubed

Not much room in here. Rub of gaberdine and newsprint.
Hiss-suck of door opening. Mind the gap.
New throng of commuters clutching plastic sandwiches and
Wilted copies of the Metro.
Now nose to tie and elbow to paunch.
Not a happy sardine.
Off at the next stop.
Unnecessary grab when sudden stop-jolt.
Standing room only.
Can't even turn round.
Need a wee.
Cold water tap running.
Trickle,
Trickle,
Trickle.
Not funny.
Shut up.

My Bed

Sink into your pocket sprung comfort and recall
The tear-damp pillowcase when Fiona died.
Cradles me as I watch the lava lamp
Gulp and clot gobs of purple and pink trip.

Notice hack cough after wheeze into a crump of a tissue;
Fight the wretch pneumonia.
No appetite; head-turn at a hearty minestrone –
Stomach churn from sweet-sour smell.

My bed saw one leg over other knee; painting toenails livid red;
Tissue woven in between my toes.
Fingers next, with a dedication to lap each nail;
Tongue escapes mouth with each application.

Write a scribble of a complaint to the phone provider,
After a heated row about the bill.
But, dear provider your tariffs stink.
Furious tapping with THE CAPS LOCK on.

And you saw me eat jalfrezi and drink rough red wine,
With a top lover from a chipped mug,
Because we were too drunk to find a glass.
Bedclothes strewn in celebration.

You are king-size in size and stature.
You know everything.

Do Not Go Gentle into That Good Night (Thank you, Dylan Thomas)

Do not go quickly into that dark night,
You're not the one who should be angry.
I'll rage, rage against the lying; you absolute shite.

Thought you, pisshead, should know I'm right
Because your words mean nothing, eh?
Do not go quickly into that dark night.

Oh God, your waving, what a sight.
You'll regret that mate, one day.
I'll rage, rage against your lying; you absolute shite.

You've been caught and now you're taking flight,
Hope you realise that, as you leave and go on you way.
And go quickly into that dark night.

You've had it now; get out of my sight,
I'm not blind and I know you've been seeing that girl, Gaye.
I'll rage, rage against the lying; you absolute shite.

And you, my friend, there in the sad night;
Don't blame me, or fight those tears, I say.
Go quickly into that sorry night, you useless piece of cheating shite.

Cold

With kohl eyes and sleeveless chill;
Gooseflesh when she orders
Avocado sandwich – with coffee to go.
Fumble for her purse.

He watches her reflection in the piano shine.
Plays on without seeing a key.
Stops to collect his duffle.
Follows her Ghost perfume.

At home, Mum peals circles of potato onto newspaper,
Long twirls of soil and eyes;
Try to form a complete skin again.
Accompanies with beheaded carrots.

Listens for her footsteps; her key in the door.
Wipes hands on her apron.
May we come in says first police officer;
With polite, professional grim.

Garage

Blue overalls draped over gaping bonnet,
Climbs further in taking one foot of the floor,
Emerges with the latest extraction.
Inspects, then wipes it on an oily rag.
Strong whiff of agreeable petrol.

Try it now barks senior. Junior twists fob and ignites engine;
Splutters to a start with clutter and a wheeze.
No problem.
Radio plays *We are the Champions* and junior punches the air.
Body robots around the car.

Go home, soft lad.
Junior unbuttons and peels off his greasy clobber.
Going home time, weekend starts.
See my mates.
Get shit-faced.

Boss reaches for his pocket, pulls out a crumpled tenner.
Have a drink on me, boy.
Heads back to his poke of an office.
Shakes his head and smiles;
Wipes his hands with a rough paper towel.

Peggie's Handbag

Contents tipped on her Formica table
Reach in to the faux silk lining of her mock-crock handbag.
Spiked by her biros; forced to huddle by a fierce elastic band,
Granddaughter's sucky orange sweet still clings to a tissue.

Tiny black and white photo : Des beams with
Fifties quiff and jaunty Christmas hat.
Leather purse rattles with £2.72 pence;
A Tesco token for chocolate Hobnobs.

And the Lotto ticket her carer had brought with her small carton of milk.
Bus tokens in the zipped bit – 5 saved for journeys to the library,
Old lady mints; hints of shopping trolleys and knitted cardigans.
A wooden hair brush bristling with candy floss hair.

And that worn True Scarlet lipstick.
She had insisted on wearing it on the ward.
The nurse said she looked so glamorous,
And she smiled, grimaced, and flinched.

She said Des was her rock.
She said she had a good life.
Didn't expect it to be so soon.
Snapped the clasp shut on Peggie's life.

Who Knew

She knew and he knew.
The trance of a glance; the fizz, the heart-pounding whizz.
She knew and he knew that averting eyes and
Looking out if the window when they met was a ruse.

She knew and he knew the brush by was deliberate.
She knew the soft feel of the nape of his neck.
He knew her flutter- sigh and gentle moan.
They both knew – yet no-one else knew.

He knew and she knew, but no-one else knew.
No-one.

Barbara

How outraged would you a be?
But I didn't lift the coffin lid.
I didn't say, 'Get up, Barbara; we have a plane to catch.'

See polite aisle shuffle, tight-lipped nods, light shoulder taps.
Thick, cream candles flicker their respect. Breathe in the smell, of a school history trip; Mr Dudgeon doling pennies for brass rubbing.
Hymn books tucked in the backs of the pews, for the pages that few know.

A gospel choir of smiling heavyweights sang tributes with gusto and rhythmic sway. Rapid blink to suppress eye well.
Waft from sweet white lilies. Glimpse of tiny cards: declaring life-long remembrance, and wishing eternal peace.

Kind eulogies, with waves of polite, laughter at odd memories of your sartorial elegance and your proclivity for dry white.

Oh, Barbara, I wish it was 11.30 in the hotel lobby, and you are suggesting a little nightcap before bed.
And we giggle and laugh about the Italian policemen who yell out 'Bella, Bella' at us, as we negotiate the Roman traffic.

Farewell, my darling Barbara, the heavens will chill the Pouilly Fume for your return home.

Millie the Dog

She's stubborn if her lead is dangled and it's raining. She plants her bum;
Won't move.

She leaves tiny pools of period blood on the floor. Refuses to wear the giant knickers – yanks them off.

When she pooed on the kitchen floor, she avoided eye contact.

And her phantom pregnancy, well, she took a toy monkey-scruff to bed and growled if anyone came close.

She laughs a lot. Throws her head back and shows her teeth when she has a tummy tickle.

And those cats – well, she hates them. Squares up to them, But runs away if they hiss.

Left she is dejected. Return and she smothers you with licks and bowls you over with devotion.

She's extraordinary.

In the Soup

I fell in.

I thrash in onion slithers; a frisbee of carrot hurls my way,

Slither of leek slaps my face like an errant plastic bag.

In the sea of barley bob, a cheeky thyme tests my knicker elastic.

There's a nuzzle of basil crouton by my nose,

And a chive wraps around my ankle.

I'm in a right stew.

Quick grab the ladle, straddle in and reach the bread board.

Oh, pepper is making me…

Bright overhead light,

Eyes wide open.

It's com…

Sne…

Sne…

Sneeze

Smile.

Spider

I saw you out of the corner of my eye.
Why are you scurrying this way?
You're the colour of kohl and
I don't want you near me.

You're too different; long spindly legs, black hunched-back.
You belong somewhere else.
Why are you trying to creep up on me?
Don't invade my space.

I'm going to squash you with this rolled up Daily Mail.
Last time I tried to flatten you, you curled up in a ball,
And you played dead.
How did you resurrect to torment me again?

I'm going to put a sign on my door.
No moths
No flies
No spiders
Go home; you're not welcome here.

Pictures

Sky scraper stuffs of popcorn; occasional grab and palm scoff.
Trail of escaped kernels in the aisles,
Mum with vat of fizz with vicious straws,
And me and her holding hands to together seats.

When we were younger, Mummy and me,
I genuflected in the aisle, and put my hand over my mouth.
The seats flipped back, and the uniformed lady guided us by torch.
Sideways squeeze, excuse me, excuse me;
Red velvet curtain opens,
Let the show begin.

Hush of anticipation, lights down,
Assault of the adverts,
Full throttle of the soundtrack; revved hard for the 'coming soon'.
Grab a nacho and slurp some coke.
I found an orange, greasy lipstick under the seat
And I drew it round like a clown.

We had ads for carpets or the local Chinese restaurant.
Always a signed certificate on the screen before the big film started.
Stir a weeny tub of vanilla ice cream until it was ready to drink.
Mum let me miss school and we were together her and me.
And she smiled and wiped my mouth with a tissue.

Now, I have to shout for her to hear, and her gnarly hands shake, and her
Skin is crepe paper.
She has a lap roast on a tray with a reek of cabbage.
And I must wipe her mouth with their rough paper towels,
But her smile is still the same.

Hot

Khaki shorts burdened with flesh– Dad, well-tattooed,
Carries two folded chairs and mismatched towels, says: 'come on, Calum.'
Boy with a flushed face, damp fringe, shiny polyester football shirt
Billows, follows with 9 on his back.
Mum zaps the car – both well upholstered; flip-flops flapping,
Plastic cool box in the crook of her arm.

Romeo attacks his mobile with a dexterous thumb.
Calum lunges at his ice-cream –
Staring at the clear, blue sky after each lick.
Doesn't want the cone, inverts it on top of the council bin;
Contents leave a creamy seepage.
'United are up 2-0 arsehole.'
'Pack it in you two.'

Towels down, sun-screen slaps
Toddler nappie-waddles to the boys – offers an orange plastic ball.
'Want a game mate?' Calum gentles, braces showing.
With a blank rethink, the baby turns, stumbles then totters back to Mum.
'He doesn't want to play with you, face-ache.'
'Shut-up, knob-head.'

Romeo and Calum watch a bikini saunter by,
Their gaze follows as she adjusts her headphones; wallows
In the attention, and smirks to herself.
'You're punching mate?' chucks Calum, as he thumps Romeo's shoulder.
A towel flicking frenzy ensues.
'Will you two cut it out,' declares Mum.

As battle ceases, more sun-cream slathers and they
Surrender to the rays, and lay prostrate to the sun.
Romeo falls asleep – Ray-Bans modelled…
The sun bakes a sandcastle, and melts ice creams – leaves
A small pool of sweat in the crack of Calum's arse.
But at least he doesn't have two white patches around his eyes
Eh Romeo – dickhead.

Round the Ward

Snatch of the cubicle curtain; walked around the bed in
One polyester swoop.
Traipse of white coats
Sling of stethoscopes, mull of medics.

Patient's face grooved with anxiety,
Pathetic arm pierced with cannula, sniff of iodine.
Water jug – green plastic lid and
Grey cardboard kidney bowl for company.

Consultant, smart threads, centre stage, scans notes.
Obs,
Meds,
Obvs,
Next.

One junior, pushes spectacles back with his middle finger,
Eyes absorb, ever keen,
Scratches his ankle –
A Bart Simpson sock exposed.

Nurse glance at fob, folds strands of hair behind her ear.
Scribble and sign, scribble and sign,
Eager to beat the trundle of the food trolley,
Linger drift of curry stirs hunger pang.

'YOU'RE NOT GOING HOME TODAY, GLADYS.'

Rheumy eyes stare back – searching explanation,

Searching,

Searching,

Searching.

Footisocky (With thanks to Lewis Carroll's Jabberwocky)

'Twas match-crush, and the blidey crudes
Did chunt and rootle in the ens:
All ruddies were the scummer ludes,
And bloosies at the elser end.

Dis ruf did blew hez wizzle hollow,
An arms did go al pointy,
His kneeze al knobbly-wallow,
Callow, callay dey was al disjointy.

The bloosies scrollowed at the ruf,
De crude wiz full besurd!
They scrollowed we huz hud enuf
Dis ruf he is a turd!l

De ruddies must ratch a scorey-match,
They weeved and dived in haste
Another goll to total-snatch,
No bloodle tim to waste!

The bloosies did one last dash,
Der forwood out at front.
The goll went in; they saw the cash
But fell and did a shunt.

The wizzle blu, come on my sin,
The bloosies goll klecked in!
Der hands wiz hi; their shirties swapped,
Dey was match champee-in!

'Twas match-crush, and the blidey crudes
Did chunt and rootle in the ens:
All ruddies were the scummer ludes,
And bloosies at the elser end.

Ip Dip Sky Blue

Shove open the double doors,
Screech, limb flail.
Chase, chase – you're it.
Pinch, punch first of the month and no return.

Brian – whiff of sour milk and flecks of crisp on his fat top lip,
Slight spit when he spoke.
Fed with hate, full of spite – paki, ginge, porker, speccy –
Executing Chinese burns and scudding wedgies.

Gaggles of girls with linked gingham arms.
Bridget whisper-lisp:
'Anyway she's not my friend anymore'
'What's the time, Mr Wolf?'

Bundles of boys, smell of scrambles,
Clamber on the British bulldog.
Collapse, howl laugh, scrape of knees,
White shirt tails flutter.

Timothy kneels on the edge of the netball court
On his own, toggled-up duffle.
Mr Happy plaster on his left leg;
Staring at bug scuttle.

Mrs Shrubsole dunks a cupped malted milk – with Amy
A need of a girl, eyes a pity –
Full of grasp.
Clings to the warmth of her teddy bear coat.

Nearby steamy kitchens burdened with aluminium crash; waft of cabbage
Scrape of giant spoons; white plates with roasted mush,
Rhubarb crumble and molten custard; corrugated skin slides into a plastic
Bowl for afters; sometimes seconds.

Mr Pierce blows a whistle,
Claps for a line up.
Grubby fingers grab eyelids – 'Guess who?'
Teeny palms swat them away – 'Get off or we will tell miss.'

At the back, hunt a runt –
Brian catching his prey with a wedge or a flick,
Always last, always friendless,
Always a bully.

Thank you, Mr Shakespeare

Shall I compare yo to me new tattoo?

Yo are more lovely, chilled and sick.

Yo blow me way; no one is as peng as you.

We'll soon be back at school; new teach is such a dick.

Bloody hot today – we'll all get burnt.

Mum is well old, she's forty two;

She dresses like a kid; she's never learnt,

Sis's a ming bint; like a hippo in the zoo.

Yo won't get old; you'll always look right fit.

You're looking well bitch; you're such a beauty,

And we will forever be and oh shit,

I've carved Liam 4 Annie in that tree.

Our names will always be there, defo be,

I swear down they will. Yo see. Yo see. Yo see.

Bedtime

My bed (aged 6 1/2)

I hate bedtime.
And the opening bars of Coronation Street.
And the blister hot or shocking cold flannel – which tap does Mum chose?
And the crisp or slightly slime-wipe on my face
And the warm milk – would prefer cola.
And cleaning the gap in my teeth. Swallowed one tooth eating mashed potato!
Dad wrote to the tooth fairy – explained a fork had pushed it out.
Still got some pennies.
But when Dad kisses me goodnight it is always too early to sleep.

I often try and make the words on my heater into different words.
So HOTPOINT becomes POT, TIP, PIN, POO and so on. I've got to 12 so far.

As my eyes close, my bed becomes a flying bed.
As it sets off, I snuggle with my teddy to stop him falling off.
Is the face on the moon real? I will fly close by to find out.
But first, I've been next door and hovered above my neighbours garden.
I saw some older kids there – they had a radio and they were… I can't tell you. Aha. I will whisper it.
Kissing.

Where the Sea Stops (For my daughter – these were her toys when she was six)

I told them not to go out.
But they had plans, I can't pretend
And the gang of friends whispered behind their hands,
And giggled and hugged, back-slappingly;
Let's find out where the sea ends.

I lined them up on my bed; backs against the wall
Do not move I said. But I know they did.
When I was shopping with my mum,
My hugging toys went to the seaside,
I'm not joking – they came back soaking.

They climbed downstairs – Jack and Sash,
And for the door they made a dash.
They wobble-stood on shoulders to reach the door handle – what a scandal.
Jack and Rups, Amadeus, Sash and Jay
Had planned to go out for the day.

With excited fur, and whiskers twitching, they opened the door;
Jack's nose was itching and he sneezed
And they tumbled to the floor.
Topped with glee,
The little animals sang – we're free.

Holding paws they crossed the road,
Passed the ice cream van
Inside the lady, not a man,

Shouted, 'Like a ninety-nine my fluffy friends.'
'We can't, we're going to find out where the sea ends.'

Ouch on the pebbles, crunch on the shingle,
The toys could feel their tiny toes tingle.
'It's there,' shouted Sash, pointing at the foam water,
'That's where it ends.'
But it kept swooshing away, it was difficult to say.

There's a patch of sand, let's have a rest
And an ice-cream that's the best.
Amadeus, already very plump,
Said I will get them and he did a hop, skip
And a jump.

So five teeny toys with an eye for adventure,
Had a great day out,
In fact, it was the best day ever in this weather.
Sash squealed that Barbie had a bikini she could borrow.
So please, please, please could they come back tomorrow?

All the Fun

Chancers dangle over backs of gilded walzers,
Dagger tatts too close to pustular girls,
Belly rings and blue damson lips;
Ready for a whizz; eager for a spin.

Tumescent skin escapes tight denim-
Crops fringed with fray.
The boom base of music churn, vies with a clamber of yobby youths;
One hirples to catch up,

Stalls bulge with fluorescent stuffed toys,
Bulls-eyes challenge Myopia,
Candied gleam of glassy toffee apples and ever so excited popcorn.
Whiff of fried onions, and vinegary chips.

Impaled horses destined to travel the same route; grin of tooth,
Oblivious to their fate, pent with stupid.
They had names you know. Dolly, Romeo, Freddy...
Would have called them Dave or Valerie. Perhaps Colin. or Mabel.

Smack of bumper cars;
Spin and rotate with frenzy like principal dancers on point
And then ram gentle souls on a Sunday drive.
No Bumping signs ahead.

Parents climb with slow precision into big wheel sway,
Check wee George is safe in harness.
He looks over whizzy rides with sulk,
Wishes he could raise his arms to defy a gut-lurch drop.

Marie Antoinette wigs of spun sugar bob past
Rifle galleries of tat,
A motley kid with a shiny tiger face,
Lashes out at a nasty wasp.

Young girls clutch each other;
Scramble on board ghost train rattle,
Scream through dangle of fluorescent skeletons;
Shriek through layers of strawberry lip gloss

Roll up, roll up.
Grab a mat, sit in a teacup, spin until you feel sick, eat a dog
And lick your fingers. All the fun,
All the fun. All the fun.

Grannie and Grampa's

Grampa is a smile of a man in beige slacks; kindness in
A cardigan. He whistles through his false teeth, and I
Bought him birthday cards with horses;
As Mum says, he sees them at the bookies.

Grannie, waft of lavender, wears a dress-tent of large flowers
And her hands smell of onions when
She squeezes your face and plants a sucker kiss.
In the kitchen, she thumps meat with a large hammer until it is flat.

My brothers and I perch on their brown Draylon sofa,
Legs brisk-swing at a sweetie tin.
Sticky tape ripped, tin prized open, Grampa teases:
'You don't like these,'
But eager fingers scatter soft centres and sticky toffees.

'Turn the telly on, Dad.'
Grampa jumps up – he's grannie's remote control.
On the black and white telly they're watching snooker.
Grannie didn't want a colour TV, as she does not like the sight of blood.
I didn't think there is much blood in snooker.

'Fetch some tea, Dad – and don't forget the doilies.'
Not sure what doilies are for, not sure adults knew either.
Then tea in spotty teacups, always with saucers and battenburg on doilies.
And us kids had tumblers fizzing with Corona orangeade.

Gran in a sudden fluster.
Kissing now on the screen, and clothes shedding.
'Change the channel, Dad.'
Room becomes full of unnecessary loud talk, and then stops with
A switch to calm monochrome football.

Supermarket

Coin in slot; jangle of the dangle,
Trolley release and off we go.
Dan's lift into his own seat, little feet slide in,
Chloe clings to the handle eyeing a Kinder egg,
Climbs for a ride; can we get some gum?
Mum's face clenched with frustration.

Aisles high with BOGOF and two for one,
Chloe offering multipack – put it back darling.
Andrew's Mum ahead; wheeling calm, hair fragrant with blow-dry.
Mum lowers her scrunch head to avoid,
Reaches for the misty frozen peas; painful to the touch.
And the dinosaur chicken – look, Dan, you like these?

Misery of the toy aisle ahead.
Can we get these? Will you buy that, Mummy?
Huge display of tiny plastic creatures;
Layers of impenetrable sharpness and difficult ties.
Massive aisle of Frozen stuff. Let it go Chloe, Mum bounces Olaf back
To his synthetic kingdom.

Here comes the confectionery; vibrant with prime,
Touch of sly, come hither sugar.
Waiting patiently, trap of lick
Clean up with the promise,
Oh, you naughty sweeties –
Waiting to trip us up with your liquorice shoelaces.

At the checkouts, wheel to the smallest queue,
Tiller puts up her plastic sign.
Go to another till. What?
All other queues twenty five people deep; zig to one
Queue and zag to another.
Chloe wailing because Mum won't buy her a sticker book.

Fluster-flicks for a card – so sorry – left it in the car;
Puce with embarrassment.
Can we leave the trolley here?
Cashier's eyebrows skim the ceiling – 'Here to help' badge at a slant.
Shopping-less traipse, Mum's lips pursed.
Baby Dan on hip, clutching Chloe's hand, dreams of some dry white.

Cape Town 1952

Mango, mango everywhere the woman go, the man go.
Burst of smilesong, glimpse of Buddha tum
Gapped-toothed fruit seller, proffers fruit
To scuttle throng; rude with rejection.

Thick billow. Sharp whistle. Flag waves.
Panic pull of knee high sock.
Run, Betty, catch this train
Before Mommy's face glowers plump beef tomato.

Door slams, fierce shoves,
Large arses win at musical chairs.
No seats, Betty, no seats
Look again.

Large lady, green dress burst, legs akimbo.
Chicken's head pokes from a hessian bag,
Soaked patches of underarm stain,
Spray from a thumbnail-gouged orange.

Betty forces way through limbs and packages,
Trips over shoes and baggages;
Arms up, through corridor choke
Hurdles bags and legs aslump.

New carriage – space to sit.
Door shut with consideration.
Calm spread of broadsheets, sniff of briefcase leather.
Monogrammed linen on the headrest.

A seat by the window – an actual seat by the window.
Upturned bug struggles to right himself
Betty pencil-flicks it over to escape, to fly away.

Eyes slowly shut with sway motion and sun kiss
Brown skin cradles in lull and comfort.

Sudden sharp sizzle like a branding-iron in her plaited hair-part.
Betty turns- the Flat-nosed man removes his trophy cigarette.
He stubbed and twisted it. Twisted it.
The man smiles; ginger eye-brows raise.

Betty alights with hurry shock; with flat nose at the window
Still smiles – beams delight.
Unfolds a Cape Town Observer
Skin pale – devoid of blood

Betty upped her pace; satchel clutch to her chest.
Steeped in well, brims with shame.
No cry, Betty; no cry, Betty.

Above the door:
Europeans Only

I Wandered Was My Shirt Too Loud (Thank you, William Wordsworth)

I wondered was my shirt too loud
And patted pockets for my fills
When all at once I saw the crowd ,
The host, of course; that Dick – Ted Hills.
Beside the club, awash with sleaze,
Punching and teasing - stupid geez.

Continuous to the bars they wind
And strut along in wide boy way,
They stretched in never-ending line
Along passed bouncers; go to pay;
Top birds saw I at a glance,
Tossing their hair in for a chance.

Inside they danced, I heard girls say
Oh let's have another Chardonnay.
I clocked that fit girl Tiffany.
But did she even notice me.
I could not stop staring, but little thought
What that evening would have brought

Next morning in my bed I lie,
I swear down; I was in a right foul mood,
I flashback to the night that I
Been for a slash then by the bar I stood;
And then my heart sinks and my pint spills,
As Tiff was dancing with that dick Ted Hills.

Remember, Remember

Boys punched and teased as they jostled their way to the front.
Mums squatted and zipped hoodies.
The sky exhaled burst upon burst of gunpowder shot
And bangers thunder-cracked the heavens
To goad yelping dogs and scaredy-cats.

Lifted chins shouted pantomime oohs and soothing ahhhs;
As Superior rockets blasted, bragged and
Fleetingly lit reflections in eager eyes.

Giggling groups of scoffing children,
Breath like burnt onions, prodded and provoked
The guy with nasty sticks.

He threw all he had at them. His news-stuffed jacket, plump sausage trousers
And mismatched socks crashed with intent and fury.
His mean fire spat sharp, spiteful flicks at their shrieking toes.

Amongst the charred cardboard his yellow plastic mask melted into a satisfied
Smile.